You Are Here
to Break Apart

Meghan Sterling

LILY POETRY REVIEW BOOKS

I looked at all the trees and didn't know what to do.
A box made out of leaves.
What else was in the woods? A heart, closing. Nevertheless.
Everyone needs a place. It shouldn't be inside of someone else.

Siken, Richard, *Detail of the Woods,* 2011.

Table of Contents

While the Eyes Seemed Closed in Sleep

she was lost in the fescue, the orchard grass
      a second skin, imagining she was a fox. Red tailed, whiskered,
wearing the hay like a crown, she went to die in it,
      to lose herself in the sun behind the silo, to stumble along
the maze of corn that led her away from the past into the past,
      where the corn was sweet off the stalk, where the silo poured
an endless spiral of seed to feed her dreaming cattle. The tractors rolling over the hills
      to the troughs, the ground wet with spill. The cattle nuzzling
her hands as she petted their cool noses, as she looked into their flat eyes
      soft as the tips of the bluestem. The land murmuring like water. At night,
she hid in her den, a quilt domed over her legs, the smell of cattle on her fingers,
      as he tried to find a fox to love, as if one could heal her, its hair like corn silk,
its barking throat. As if a fox could love. What makes a fox a fox, says the field,
      says the cattle as they settle deep into the byre, is that it only seems to sleep.

Dear Memory

Between chores, a shadow I follow

to the field. Beside the creek,

a brown snake, writhing in switchgrass.

The still water jumping with bugs,

their delicate wings, their legs thin as pins.

The fear of the snake, then the closeness

of water, shivering the grass

in a breeze warm as a cow's tongue,

bugs dancing along the water's skin,

my hesitation. Dear memory,

what would you have me do?

The bugs dragged lines behind them

as they skittered, the water's lip trembling.

The snake forgotten. The snake a monster

crouching in the grass. Already,

I can hear my family beginning to move

in the house behind me. Already, I am doing

the wrong thing. There are beds to weed.

There are clothes to pin to the line. But

the blue of the shallow creek is dimpled

with bugs like a thousand shooting stars,

dipping themselves into the silk. The clouds darken.

I hear my grandmother bellowing it's time for dinner

as shadows amble to the house. The bugs move,

alert to the sensation of water. My fingers,

electric with desire. My fingers, already touching

the water. My grandmother, my name now a shriek

of impatience. The door slams open. Wait just a moment,

memory. There is something of myself here,

in this water, in my fingers, searching the water's surface, blind.

In the snake that has moved away.

How July

was a tangle of bluestem, fireflies storming their prayers
against the barn siding, fields lit as though burning,
night loud with cicadas shouting accusations, pokeberry

stains left by the birds across the porch steps,
smearing the bottoms of our sandals a black purple
like the bog croaking at the periphery of pasture

we could feel against our bare arms, a stranger's breath.
Then morning, faint wind, the day yawning open
against the sky's sullen scowl, an endless lawn to mow

in heat that shivers green in awareness of itself
like an adolescent, scent of manure and grandmother
at the kitchen window, her fury searing the back of my hair,

like the brush pile near the creek bed under the magnifying glass.
How July was penance for some crime that had taken place in the womb,
before knowledge, in a forgotten bowl of school and bedtime and bare feet

padding the hallway, how July was where I chained myself
to absence, my body becoming smoke that hovered above
the slaughtering sheds, their metal roofs singed with old fires,

their chimneys slatted and slattern and barely hinged, their axes
rusting but for the leather handles that fit close to the palm,
ready for the surrendering neck of the wood.

In the Box of Old Photos, a Yellowing Polaroid

In this one, she leans over,
as if he is all that keeps her from falling,

her face turned away. The landscape of summer
behind them. He looks past the camera into a future

round as a clockface, another moon
eclipsed in the hand he holds at his side.

The watch on his wrist. Her floral dress
light on her body, like the perfume of lilac trees.

Farmland behind the windows. A sound of shaded water
filling the cistern. I didn't know them then,

this was before. Days of hot sky barely touched by clouds.
Then sudden rain. In this version, they always are this:

her weight against his steady frame. His frame
heavy as hooves in the barnyard. He looks off,

past the camera. Their hair long and full. The clock
ticking off minutes in a hallway full of books. Football

on the radio. The faintest echo of storm. She leans on his body,
his distance, his remove. He looks past the camera.

You Could Cut It with a Knife

When the woman speaks, the knife enters the room,
its blade bloodied with raspberry jam. There's the hay smell
of rural fields, where we fled from the city, where we gathered
pails full of berries one summer, while the next, barren bushes
stared vaguely, pantry shelves emptying of last year's harvest,
when all was dark rings on wax paper, a white moth's wings
under a light. My daughter may never learn where the canning
jars are kept or know the cedar scent of the studio in the jade-dark
summer with its tea kettle and stream heavy with the cistern's
spillover, engorged and winding like a queen's dark hair, the sun
growing hotter and closer as an old man's hungry and unwanted
mouth. She may never know the darkness of dim woods, foxfire's
light drawing the beetles near. Everything may be gone by the time
she can remember scent, by the time she is ready to be alone with
the ghosts in the grass. Once a man lived here who pulled tree trunks
like a mule—the fence he made still stands, and rings the garden, echoing
the past like an old well. Once this place was rented to hoarders who filled it
with knick-knacks and tissue box covers. Once a shotgun blast burst a hole
in the asbestos siding. Once this place had heard the rage uttered beneath
a woman's breath as she counted the ways her husband had stripped her
like petals of the Larkspur eaten to lace by the rainbow flurry of Japanese
beetles. Once this place had known the crease of the knife held tight in a fist,
blood like jam on the farmhouse floor. When the woman speaks, the house
rattles its poplar bones. When the woman speaks, the knife trembles to find flesh,
comes back on itself.

Mirror

The monster in the room, tall as a door, framed
        in wood. Why did I want you here, watching?
I thought I could winnow mother out of my face,
        prune father out of my teeth, smooth my ancestors
out of my hair, grown wild as weeds. Woman now,
        I stand there growing in all the wrong directions,
all of us changing like 100 words for snow, all compelled
        by forces big as the rope that tethers the moon.
How many times I have hoped I had arrived and was still at sea.
        I tell myself: I must submerge like Ophelia, floating on flowers
towards her fate. I want to say our fates will be different.
        I want to say I will age like silver, tarnishing gently,
but I feel the longing to fight, wrestle, force time to say uncle
        as it gasps on the floor. The days that pass etch my skin like glass
in the same troughs my mother bears, burrowing like stones
        that wear holes in my pockets, razing whole houses, like the one
we found deep in the woods, making love
        on the crumbled foundation, undies down around ankles,
Spanish moss draping like surrender over the wide arms of the oaks
        that stood in mute witness. Finding old glass in the wreckage,
pieces of silver had vanished from the edges, revealing stones,
        grass, dirt, where my face was the face of a child through a cloud
and that was years ago. How the trees have left us, the forests
        razed for lumber, the fields picked clean of fescue and smooth beneath
the empty houses. And when I went to the edge of the latest murder and gripped
        its vinyl siding, my face in the whiskered glass.

Says the Stone

Only fragments of the story remain—
lamp, stone, smash, wall, head, ash.

I don't know where I was when I learned it—
where the blunt fist was born. Where the rage.

How memory stores its knives for later use.
The places the briars go, their little snags.

All the hurt like a tangle of thorns,
and no way through but through. Even the house,

with its panes of glass, with its metal blinds tied
with a cord—a weapon. When did I begin to flinch?

I found my solitude beneath the sawn-off blades
of oaks, a small circle away from the grief of razed fields.

Away from the sun's eye, I became the fox. The woods
and their cool floor, my cheek to the dark and shadow.

Drawing the earth with my finger. The stone coming.
Says the stone in my ear, *you were born here.* A seed spent

in darkness, in dreams. If only you can remember
the sound.

Lineage

Once I begged to be back in your body.
I summoned your fingers to my neck,
wrapped myself in the curl of your knuckles.
Once I was inside the stone of your finger
that pointed South, to the thicket of poplars and fir,
that time we tried to make a home out of scraps
of cloth, slats of wood, when even the birds fled
the chimney, when even the moths kept away
from the wool. When I was a child, I spoke
as a fly, I spoke as a seed splits for the approaching bird.
Once I wound myself in the web of your mooring,
a thread that came undone and couldn't relearn the weave.
How I became the auxiliary to your wheel,
the brunt of your thumb's down, the weight of your words
like a barrow's. Once I learned how to look away
from what was coming, loving the shadow that fell.

O, Holy

And we sang when winter brought our faces closer
to the dark, our ears pressed to the white wood of balsam,

cut quick and boughed, and the moon was a glass held to
mouths that could no longer taste, and the moon was milk

we spilled to watch run to the corners of the room.
And the ice wet stars out of the dark house.

And the cold cut to the skin of the earth hard with frost.
And the colored lights strung along the kitchen window

spattered with dish soap in a pattern of flowers, and
the leaked light along the frozen creek guiding us

towards the woodpile to fetch sticks for burning.
And the candles lit beneath the damask of the sky.

And the fir tree at an angle with icicles trailing off
the terminal buds. And the singing in the gravel road.

And the hands plunged into pockets fat with feathers.
And the rustling of zippers and ripstop above skittering legs.

And the sound of my father running. And the sound of my
father happy.

Self-Portrait on Hike with Father and Cicadas

There are birds where there should be bells, scree
where there should be sky, the song of cicadas' alarm,
and I was all elbows and salt, wet from wandering
in the creek, sodden as the farm fields were at the edges.

Remember my heels plunging the mud. Remember my voice
before it began to shake. There were bones where there should be flesh,
flesh where there should be air. I never quite fit with the starlings,
more a sparrow, more a wren. *More bird than belle,* the mirror said.

My father in silent lead, his binoculars around his neck like a noose.
How I stumbled. How I fell. How I followed him anywhere.
Wading across the creek, the scuttling of snakes in the grass,
the cicadas in the reeds. Cicadas in synchronized weeping,

indignant as we carved our way across their creek, waist-deep.
My bird legs, my mouth, flush with silt, three feet beneath green water,
skirted with bugs in their shivering circles, graceful as figure skaters.
The wall of brush. My father, our guide across murk, its ceiling of scrub.

Emerging onto a field with its blanket of stones. Remember
the catbird chorus, miles from any church. Miles from the kitchen
with its double bowl sink, from women and their impatient, unnamable want.
The glare that day was from the sun, its glowering red, its preferable heat.

Give Us This Day

We gather together always. The tea towels
wing their way to the table, their reds and blues
against a pane of white, all stains and creases,
folded beneath hands that ache to shape themselves
into prayer. But we don't pray at this table,
not to heaven, but sometimes to a God
that can harmonize this chorus, sail this day
into unspoiled blue: no hunger, no threat,
just light and sky and the plum jam hidden beneath
the basement step. Meanwhile, the men are hollering
for food, the women are cursing them, the way they expect,
the way women deliver to them, giving up on themselves.
Breakfast like a forest fire contained in ceramic bowls,
the years left like cinders under the table for the dog.
The family's chairs creak in a fit like a ghost in the attic.
The porridge bubbles over. The broom falls behind the door.
The coffee streaks the pot black and a curse sails over
the room like a bird to its branch.

The Way Back

was slower, those Saturday drives past farms and Walmarts,

through Coffee County or Franklin, the corn a bit greener

to the West, the soybeans nearer the ground, tumbling

like morning glories under a sky trimmed close as a hedge.

Raindrops would dot the windshield. The slap of the wipers.

I would consider who we were before we knew each other,

how my body had rebelled against being loved, how I would

look over these fields as a fox does its hole and imagine

each seed like a lima bean in a jar, sprouting one green leaf.

Also I would consider: the rust of the tiller, the farmer at

the wheel, whether he made his bed in the morning, whether

someone else was in it when he left to begin. The lilac dawn.

The smell of the cattle rising out of the barns. Whether I would

be a farmer's wife, straining the whey out of the curdled milk,

gathering eggs, callouses on my large, sure hands. I wondered

over at my mother, driving the car in quiet, the gray sky outside

the window like a field of snow. What more did she want of these

fields, these anonymous houses with their garden plots and clotheslines.

What more did she want of the drives we took to get out of Grandmother's

house, away from the demands of men, whether my silence was as much

of a disappointment as everything else, the antique shops smelling of rain,

the kindling left out, too wet that night to burn.

Names for Ghosts

Of Winchester, Lynchburg, Manchester, Tullahoma, Walmart,
Tractor Supply and Hammer's, Jack Daniel's and George Dickel

gathering dust in the backs of tall cupboards, or the hard edges of wire
fences with cattle hair caught in barbed tufts, fences in rectangles that line

the outskirts of town, just beyond the fields planted thick with soybeans.
Of abandoned balers. Of El Taqueria and the Tyson Chicken Coops,

the scratch of the pullets, Combines tawny with grain, vegetable plots smaller
each year, columbines, foxglove, the rusting Ford in the driveway beside

the collapsed tobacco barn, or the silo silhouetted at sunset, its rush of grain
down the chute. Of the butcher at Bates, Dinah Shore Boulevard and Ethel,

Carolyn, Darwin, Odelle, Sid and Gene, Lyle, Mr. Tabb, Ruby, Tom, or the farm
next door, the barns' jagged boards slick with rot, swept clear and home

to a trailer, some horses penned into a pasture where the corn used to grow.
Where we led my brother and shrank back into cornsilk. All gone. Even

their names. Benny. Giles. Harold. Of men, and sweat, and denim coveralls
and boots wet with muck. Of women and biscuits and the entryway

caked with mud. Of the sour smell of milk in the dairy barn, its sticky floor,
its steaming hose. Of rusted nails planted deep in the dirt.

Tim's Ford Dam

Trust the light that comes over the eastern hill,
       dim as an echo, shivering the lake
       behind the cedar trees, with its pontoon boats,
       its solitude and fisherman. Remember the houses

under the surface, buried in water these 60 years.
       Once, as you swam, the light filtered gold into
       green water. You saw a trout swimming an illuminated path.
       You saw how beautiful detritus could be—a truck

10 feet deep now a bed for the fish, the broken windows
       a rusted archway to dart beneath. Soda cans glinting like jewels
       in the reeds. The center of tires along the banks filling with ferns.
       Trust that the light knows what you need to see—cemetery

half hidden in weeds as the sun rose like a duck off the water's smooth belly.
       Once, the name of a relative etched into forgotten stone.
       Once, an old foundation, a mirror intact and staring up through trees.
       Once, your own hands. Trust that beneath your skin,

you are more than what they make you out to be—
       all curls and bony legs, all stumbling mouth and hands
       not good for much. That in the light, all will become clear—
       gold shining under the rims of closed eyes, gold shining

around a halo of impossible hair. That the light will illuminate what it is that you are.

Aperture

This is where we arrived each year: boardwalks across swamp,
stink of dead crabs sunk in the marsh, Spanish moss like veils

hiding the faces of all the trees. I would whisper, *we would go blind*
if we saw their sorrow. We would die of it. I knew there were secrets,

I had found the newspaper clippings, heard mention the words *murder,*
madness. My aunt as a child drawing her family without mouths, without eyes,

screaming soundlessly, as though words would do nothing but shatter the dishes
displayed in the hutch. I tell you this because I want you to know

all the things, the way history watches, like a mirror left in an abandoned house,
like grass on a grave. Every year, our birthday parties were held on the island

built with poured cement at the center of the swamp. We'd hide in the holes
left by the diggers to kiss or try a cigarette. My mother would stare into the forest,

her love hidden, woven like braids into the mangroves' tendrils. How silent
she kept at the swamp, a coin tossed into its nexus, wishes made each year

with a hollow echo bouncing off the muck as I grew longer and more afraid
of what she was hiding. How each year I crept those boardwalks

as though circling into the center of the conch, crawling to the only place
that could sound into the darkness, words the only way in, the only way out.

What We Do To Each Other

Fox darts behind the brush pile. Since the field is lush from recent
rain, the meadowgrass hides what's left behind. Glass shards.
A rusted rake. The spools of summer unwound and piled
like a cairn at a burial. There are many barrows. Mole mounds.
The old hole where the groundhog bullied the fields and sparrows—
tapping its fists at the panes to get the apple barrels. A shrine to
its body, gone these 20 years. A shrine to the orchard with its wizening
trees, trunks arcing towards earth. Once, a copperhead dozing
between the slats of the shed, bronze as rust, thick coils tight
between planks. This is how the mind works, how it gets stuck
between thoughts, a snake caught in a nap among boards, the wind
rustling as the fox takes its aim with the hoe and prays for courage.
The fox shouldn't flinch-- killing is simple, what we do to each other.
What mother would do, watching from the window. But the hoe drops
to the grass. The snake sleeps undisturbed. While the fox slinks away to its hole,
its tail a shade of shame. Unwilling to defend its turf, unwilling to fox.

Lien

There is memory in the way the sky glares
its white eyes at the heat of us, in the thunder
that creeps behind the swinging doors of the barn,
the flag that half-masts limply across air while we wait

in stillness for something to happen. There is memory
in the way a mother holds her hands as if the child
is still there, weight of an apple, a melon, bag of flour,
standing on the porch in all her emptiness, the air heavier

where once the hands were always holding. There is a room
behind a room where the photographs stare at poplar walls.
There is a sunflower seed pecked to shell by the beak of the blackbird.
There is a house the family may lose where the floor rattles its thunder

with every step. There is memory buried under the house, left in a box
made of barn wood, a medallion nested in the ashes of a beloved dog,
where the box is opened just as the wind picks up, blowing the past out
to dim the faces of the yarrow with the dead's bright dust.

You Are Here to Break Apart

And all that is ruin of flower, of the drilled well,
the layer of rubble left in the cornfields, now pasture
for neighbor's cattle, bones of the spent nickel raked
into piles, nuzzled by the Holstein out in the singed grass,
a ring of fire at night for the hunters seeking coyotes'
bodies to pile, pyre. Blood mouthed calls of the coyotes
tearing apart a single cow, the gunshots the next night
in retribution. And time like a bullseye painted on the side
of an oak, its leaves dry in what used to be spring.
All that was bullet, ruin of the road that carried
milk to the markets in Chattanooga, the hunters' stands
in the trees like magpie's nests with their treasures—
porn magazines, ammunition, crushed cans of Sundrop
and moonpie wrappers, sun faded camo baseball caps
and a shattered pair of binoculars. And a knife, its point
like the brown of a cow's eye, lit as a lake at dawn, distant
as a father, as much in the past as beauty ever was,
eye of water, of gathering cloud.

Acknowledgments

"Aperture" was published as "Birthday Parties" in *UCity Review*

"Dear Memory" was published in *Colorado Review*

"While the Eyes Seem Closed in Sleep" was published as "Finding the Fox" in *Lily Poetry Review*

"Give Us This Day" was published in *The Los Angeles Review*

"How July" was published in *Valparaiso Poetry Review*

"O Holy" was a finalist in *Gigantic Sequins* Annual Poetry Contest, 2021

"Names for Ghosts" was published in *UCity Review*

"Lien" was published in *Equinox*

"Lineage" was published in *The West Review*

"Says the Stone" was published in *Radar Poetry*

"Self-Portrait on Hike with Father and Cicadas" was published in *Idaho Review*

"Mirror" was published as "Silverback" and won *Equinox's* Annual Poetry Contest, 2021

"The Way Back" was nominated for a 2021 Pushcart Prize and published in *Mockingheart Review*

"Tim's Ford Dam" was published as "And Every Dawn" in *Mudfish 23*

"You Could Cut It with a Knife" was published in *Tusculum Review*

Multi-Pushcart Nominee Meghan Sterling (she, her, hers) has been published or has work forthcoming in *Meridian, Hunger Mountain, The Los Angeles Review, Rhino Poetry, Rattle, Colorado Review* and many other journals. She has been a Hewnoaks Fellow and a Dibner Fellow. Her first full length collection *These Few Seeds* (Terrapin Books) came out in 2021 and was an Honorable Mention for the 2022 Eric Hoffer Grand Prize in Poetry. Her chapbook, *Self Portrait with Ghosts of the Diaspora* (Harbor Editions), her second full length collection, *View from a Borrowed Field,* which won the Paul Nemser Poetry Prize (Lily Poetry Review) and her third full-length collection, *Comfort the Mourners* (Everybody Press) all came out in 2023. She lives in Maine with her family, works as a professional writer and teaches poetry workshops. Read her work at meghansterling.com.

www.ingramcontent.com/pod-product-compliance
Lightning Source LLC
Chambersburg PA
CBHW030529130626
46549CB00007B/3160